Geese on the Farm
by Mari C. Schuh

Consulting Editor: Gail Saunders-Smith, Ph.D.

Consultant: Cary J. Trexler, Ph.D., Assistant Professor
California Agricultural Experiment Station
University of California, Davis

Pebble Books

an imprint of Capstone Press
Mankato, Minnesota

Pebble Books are published by Capstone Press
151 Good Counsel Drive, P.O. Box 669, Mankato, Minnesota 56002
http://www.capstone-press.com

1 2 3 4 5 6 08 07 06 05 04 03

Library of Congress Cataloging-in-Publication Data
Schuh, Mari C., 1975–
    Geese on the farm / by Mari C. Schuh.
    p. cm.—(On the farm)
    Summary: Photographs and simple text describe geese and the lives they live
on the farm.
    Includes bibliographical references and index.
    ISBN 0-7368-1662-3 (hardcover)
    1. Geese—Juvenile literature. [1. Geese.] I. Title. II. Series: Schuh, Mari C.,
1975– . On the farm.
SF505.3.S39 2003
636.5′98—dc21   2002009674

Note to Parents and Teachers

The On the Farm series supports national science standards related to life science. This book describes and illustrates domestic geese and their lives on the farm. The photographs support early readers in understanding the text. The repetition of words and phrases helps early readers learn new words. This book also introduces early readers to subject-specific vocabulary words, which are defined in the Words to Know section. Early readers may need assistance to read some words and to use the Table of Contents, Words to Know, Read More, Internet Sites, and Index/Word List sections of the book.

Table of Contents

Geese are large birds.

Some geese are wild.
Other geese live on farms.

Geese have a strong bill and a long neck.

A male is a gander.
A female is a goose. A
young goose is a gosling.

Geese live mostly in pens or fenced pastures.

Some farmers raise geese for their meat and feathers.

Some farmers raise geese to eat weeds.

Geese eat grass and grain.

Geese honk.

Words to Know

bird—a warm-blooded animal that has feathers and wings and can lay eggs

feather—a light, fluffy body part that covers a bird's body; goose feathers often are used in pillows, sleeping bags, and bedding because they are light and keep in heat.

grain—the seed of a cereal plant; farmers feed corn and other grains to geese; farmers also feed geese soybeans, vitamins, and minerals.

pasture—land that animals use for grazing

pen—a small, fenced-in area for animals; geese live mostly outside in pens; they also have other shelter during cold weather.

weed—a plant that grows where it is not wanted; geese will eat only certain kinds of weeds.

wild—not tamed by people; some geese are wild and are not kept on farms.

Read More

Cooper, Jason. *Canada Goose.* Life Cycles. Vero Beach, Fla.: Rourke Publishing, 2002.

Miller, Sara Swan. *Waterfowl: From Swans to Screamers.* Animals in Order. New York: Franklin Watts, 1999.

Saunders-Smith, Gail. *The Farm.* Field Trips. Mankato, Minn.: Pebble Books, 1998.

Internet Sites

Track down many sites about geese.
Visit the FACT HOUND at *http://www.facthound.com*

IT IS EASY! IT IS FUN!

1) Go to *http://www.facthound.com*

2) Type in: 0736816623

3) Click on "FETCH IT" and FACT HOUND will find several links hand-picked by our editors.

Relax and let our pal FACT HOUND do the research for you!

Index/Word List

bill, 9
birds, 5
eat, 17, 19
farmers,
  15, 17
farms, 7
feathers, 15
female, 11
fenced, 13
gander, 11

gosling, 11
grain, 19
grass, 19
honk, 21
large, 5
live, 7, 13
long, 9
male, 11
meat, 15
neck, 9

other, 7
pastures, 13
pens, 13
raise, 15, 17
some, 7,
  15, 17
strong, 9
weeds, 17
wild, 7
young, 11

Word Count: 69
Early-Intervention Level: 11

Credits

Heather Kindseth, series designer; Patrick D. Dentinger, book designer;
Deirdre Barton, photo researcher

Capstone Press/Gary Sundermeyer, cover, 4, 14, 16, 18, 20
Metzer Farms/John Metzer, 1, 10, 12
Visuals Unlimited/Mark E. Gibson, 6; Bill Beatty, 8